Bright Blessings

Spiritual Thoughts, Inspirational Quotes
and Philosophical Observations on Life.

from Helen Leathers

ISBN 978-0-9558571-1-9

A catalogue record for this book is available from the British Library.

First Published in 2009 by Spreading The Magic
www.stmpublishing.co.uk

Spreading The Magic, P.O. Box 80, Church Stretton, Shropshire SY6 9AD

Cover Design by Titanium Design Ltd.
www.titaniumdesign.co.uk

For those moments when you think you need to talk,
but you may just need to listen.

Bright Blessings

FOREWORD

Having been fortunate to have spent many an hour discussing all things spiritual with Helen, I know the depth of knowledge and understanding she has over a vast range of subjects, and now, through this book, you will be able to share in that knowledge too.

Like may others I have been regularly inspired by her insightful writings, full of perception and spiritual advice, sent to me via the excellent 'Spreading the Magic' newsletters. Helen has a way of making important, and often complex subjects accessible to all by writing in a manner which is both relevant and refreshingly fun. Helen's writings are always thought-provoking whilst, thankfully, not preaching in any way.

The idea to put all of these wonderful writings from her newsletters together in one book is inspired in itself. This is a book to keep at hand, read straight through or dip in and out of as needed. This is a book to pick up and read when you are in need of a spiritual uplift, wise words or inspiration. It is a book we all need in these busy times, to help us connect, or re-connect, with our spiritual selves.

Bright Blessings,
Diane

Co-author of 'Help! I Think I Might Be Psychic. 101 Frequently Asked Question About Spiritual, Psychic & Spooky Stuff.'

CONTENTS

ABOUT THE AUTHOR

From as far back as I can remember I have seen and communicated with Spirit. Our family home had a number of ghosts, one of which was a wonderful gentle nurse from the early 1900's. When I was four I had had whooping cough, followed by chicken pox, as had my two year-old brother, and much to my mother's horror, my dad also went down with chicken pox. Mum had been up every night for weeks and was exhausted. Then along came what seemed like a miracle, a whole night of uninterrupted sleep. She came in to see me in the morning and said how pleased she was that we had all slept so well. I hadn't, I told her, but a lady in a blue dress had come in and pulled the covers back over me and I went back to sleep after that. Luckily, I do seem to inherit this ability from my mum so although a little perturbed, she mentally thanked 'the lady' for helping out and letting her catch up on some sleep. Many years later my younger sister also saw the lady who appeared to awaken her from a particularly nasty nightmare. She gave a far better description leading us to believe that the lady had been a nurse. 'The Lady', as we refer to her, obviously continues to care for children in the afterlife.

Seeing, hearing and sensing ghosts, prophetic dreams and trusting my intuition and inner guidance to avoid potentially negative situations were all a part of my life from very early on. I had devoured all of Doris Stokes' books on mediumship well before I was 12. I started reading Tarot when I was 14 and also discovered a natural ability for dowsing with a pendulum. I attended courses and workshops whenever I could from the age of 18 and found a deep affinity with crystals and the native pagan culture of the British Isles. I trained as an alternative therapist and became a Reiki Master. I loved Reiki straight away and knew without a doubt that I had to teach others about it. The self-empowerment, the wonderful healing stories, and the changes that it facilitates in people are all amazing. I started running courses as soon as I could and continue to do so, seeking to make it as accessible to everyone as possible.

Over the years my psychic side became more prevalent and I also realised how empathic I was. I feel the emotions of others, the joy, the fear, and the pain. This can be difficult sometimes but I'm also able to see their potential, which is inspiring. Throughout my twenties I worked closely with friends of like mind, some much more experienced and some at a similar point to me. We discovered more and more about ourselves, our abilities and how to tap into our inner power and knowledge. We debated spiritual philosophy and universal mysteries long into the night. I continued to do card readings and dowsing but also developed other skills including psychometry and Mediumship. I was invited to join a psychic development circle where I met and started working with Diane (my co-author for 'Help! I Think I Might Be Psychic') and others. I found that I was drawn to and had the ability to do 'rescue work'. In layman's terms this is performing something like an exorcism, a horrible phrase conjuring many negative and scary images, but one that most people will understand. Basically I'm good at getting rid of unwanted and problem ghosts. A haunted antique cauldron being the first and most unusual situation that I came across.

At 30 I relocated to Shropshire I found myself with a very definite purpose. I *had* to share my acquired knowledge and understandings with a larger audience. I was running workshops and a website for personal, spiritual and psychic development and had also started writing. Books began to take shape and I knew this was the next step for me.

My journey so far, punctuated by many paranormal experiences, has been a massive learning and development process, and I continue in this every day. I know that I'm connected to the Universe as many seeming coincidences continue to put me in front of the right person at the right time, in a better place, or out of harm's way. I don't consider myself to be special, I have simply chosen to actively pursue this avenue, to open to and connect with the Universe and to develop my own natural abilities, to ask more questions and look for more answers. I enjoy helping others to do the same, Spreading The Magic.

INTRODUCTION

In 2005 I started an online newsletter as part of a larger vision to encourage people to think about life and themselves in a more spiritual way. I had heard so many people, during courses, workshops and general conversation say that they really wished they had more time to think about 'these things' but that basically, life got in the way. So my newsletter would drop into their 'inbox' every few weeks, offering a reminder of their desire to embrace a more spiritual outlook, take more time for themselves and to give them some simple tasks to remind them of their truly spiritual nature.

I love my life and I believe that integrating the spiritual side of me into my life makes it perfect. That, for me, is the magic. So I want to reach out and help others to find the magic in themselves and in life, and for them to then spread the magic by doing the same for others.

Now that my newsletters have been pulled together in a new form, I hope that this book will serve as a point of reference and inspiration for those of us who need it, those for whom life gets in the way. Because, here's the thing, life doesn't get in the way. Life is. And if you want it to be a happy and more fulfilling one then it can be, you simply have to make that choice

This not a book designed to be read from beginning to end in one sitting. It is a book that you can dip into whenever you wish, or need to. I hope that it provides food for thought, inspiration, enlightenment and maybe a smile on occasion. Turn to this book when you need a moment of thought and contemplation, perhaps a focus on which to meditate, some philosophical help or support or as a reminder of our interconnectedness with others and with the universe.

I hope that this book will help you to get in the flow of life, to open your mind to new ideas and challenges, to develop your sense of contentment and of purpose, to find your bigger vision and to dare to dream.

I believe that everyone has the power to turn their dreams into reality and I hope that through this book you can be inspired to do just that.

By The Way...

By writing in this way, I do not wish to portray myself as an expert in anything, or that my beliefs or opinions are the right and only way, they are simply mine. They may change in time, after all, who says you have to hold the same ideas forever? If what I write resonates with you, great, if not, ignore it. My hope is that it will help you to develop your own understandings and belief system whilst being accepting and understanding of those of others.

Be the best version of *you* that you can, but be *you* no matter what, because we are all unique and perfect right now.

Bright Blessings to you all on your journey.
Helen

"The journey to wholeness begins with a single step. By allowing the magic to happen, you open yourself to your true, eternal, perfect nature."
Hazel Raven, 'Crystal Healing. A Vibrational Journey Through The Chakras'

3 Quotes About
'Journeys'

*'A journey of a thousand miles begins
with a single step'*

Confucius

*'To get through the hardest journey we need take
only one step at a time, but we must keep stepping'*

Chinese proverb

*'The journey to personal freedom can
only be achieved if you listen
to the voice of your soul'*

Michael Teal

SEASONAL SIGNS

I initially based my newsletters around the eight major traditional celebrations of the British Isles. There are a number of reasons for this. Personally I have always been drawn to our indigenous pagan beliefs and I feel saddened that while many who are interested in spiritual teachings seek knowledge in the native American or Eastern cultures, very few seem to look at what has been trampled underground in our own. Worse than that, it has been very successfully demonised by a variety of groups of people over many years. But far from indicating that we are all worshipping a horned devil, those of us that align ourselves with the cycles of nature and celebrate our more ancient calendar are no different to any other indigenous culture, or individual following any spiritual belief system.

These writings and observations of the turning cycles of the year may help you to understand your own natural rhythms and how to realign yourself with nature and tune into the living, turning, energetic universe.

The dates of these celebrations may vary depending on the source. These traditions have mostly been passed down orally through the centuries and therefore liable to have altered somewhat. The solstices and equinox dates vary because the earth does not take *exactly* 365 days to go around the sun. The extra few hours and the subsequent leap years cause the difference.

1st August - Lammas / Lughnassadh
20th -22nd September - Autumn Equinox
31st October - Samhain, All Hallow's Eve or Halloween
20th - 22nd December - Winter Solstice
1st / 2nd February - Imbolc
20th - 22nd March - Spring Equinox or Ostara
1st May - Beltane
20th - 22nd June - Summer Solstice

There are many books that go into much more detail about the 'wheel of the year', as it is known and I hope that this one will inspire you to find out more. There is no reason for where I begin our journey through the year, other than the fact that it was coming up to Lammas when I began writing my newsletters.

IT'S HARVEST-TIME
LAMMAS OR LUGHNASSADH, 1st August

The 1st of August is associated with the beginning of the harvests. The medieval Christian name for the festival held at this time of year was Lammas, meaning 'Loaf-Mass'. This refers to the breads that were baked with the first grain harvest. This is also a traditional time of year for country fairs and outdoor games.

As the days begin to shorten we too can take stock. Make a list of all the things you have achieved. Be honest, and be proud of yourself. Give yourself the opportunity to celebrate them. It's also time to think about what we would like to 'sow' or improve on for the future.

Make the most of the sun's energy as it continues to 'ripen the fruits'. Use this seasonal energy to create a vision or make plans for the future. Or simply enjoy it's warmth, feel that same warmth inside yourself and feel content with your harvest, knowing that you can achieve whatever you desire.

This is a great time of year for a family day out, why not visit a maize maze, especially with kids,. Alternatively visit a corn circle or an ancient site such as Silbury Hill in Wiltshire.

If you do nothing else...

We are all spiritual beings but we do get caught up in the mechanics of living, working etc. That can't be helped and it's okay, but we do sometimes need reminding of 'who we are' don't we? Here are 3 simple things, which if you do nothing else in the next 6 weeks, you should schedule into your life. Book time to be with the magical part of you and you will shine. So, if you do nothing else, between now and 21st of September,

1) Find a book that you have been meaning to read for ages (there's probably one on your shelf right now) and book time out to start it, even if is only half an hour.

2) Go outside into nature. Take a walk, sit and meditate, watch the clouds go by or let yourself get rained on!

3) Using the list of achievements that you made, start a gratitude journal. Basically this is like a diary of all the things you have to genuinely be thankful for. Add to it often and re-read it if you are having a bad day to remind you of all the positive things in your life.

Go on then - put them in your diary now.

"Everyone must take time to sit and watch the leaves turn"
Elizabeth Lawrence

THE AUTUMN EQUINOX
MABON, 20th-22nd September

The Autumn Equinox falls between the 20th and 22nd of September. It's the 2nd time in the year when day and night are equal but after this Equinox the nights become longer as winter gets closer. It's time to start turning inwards, allowing yourself time for contemplation and planning. Who are you? Who do you wish to be? How can you improve yourself and make steps towards being that person?

I love this time of year, there is a subtle, yet tangible buzz in the air as summer begins to slide away towards winter. The sun is still bright but there is that edge. It's not even about the temperature it's just something different that tells you it's Autumn. It's as though something exciting is about to happen. Why not go out for a walk on a windy evening, really tune into the energy of the season, embrace that exciting feeling of potential and expectation, and take it with you.

I also love the food that we get at this time of year, apples, corn and root vegetables, and taking time to make soups and apple pies. Cooking is magical. It is simple magic that anyone can do, combining a set of ingredients, initiating a change in their structure and creating a very different end result. My hint when it comes to cooking would be to never do it when you are in a bad mood. Who knows someone who has said that they love kneading dough, because they can take out all of their frustrations on it? DON'T DO THAT! I believe that what you put into the food is absorbed by those who eat it. So why not give that a go? Not the anger part, but bake or cook with love and a positive intention and see if it works for you. Calmly creating the kids meal may well give you calmer kids?? I don't know if it will but why not try? It can't hurt.

"Live your life from your heart. Share from your heart. And your story will touch and heal people's souls."

Melody Beattie

If you do nothing else...

We are all spiritual beings but we do get caught up in the mechanics of living, working etc. That can't be helped and it's okay, but we do sometimes need reminding of 'who we are' don't we? Here are 3 simple things, which, if you do nothing else in the next 6 weeks, you should schedule into your life. Book time to be with the magical part of you and you will shine. So, if you do nothing else, between now and 31st of October,

1) Go outside on a clear night and look at the stars. Breathe in the night air and look at the constellations. Perhaps you could spend a bit longer and find out more about them, or take someone with you and make a romantic evening of it.

2) Do some home baking and invite friends and family to help you eat it - apple pie is great at this time of year.

3) SMILE - go on, you can do that right now! Now just keep right on doing it. Smile at everyone, you'll be amazed at the difference it makes, even if they think you're odd, you'll feel great! (I got brilliant feedback on this one when I put it into my newsletter and it's so easy).

Go on then - put them in your diary now.

HAPPY HALLOWEEN!

SAMHAIN, 31st October

It's said that, at Halloween, the veil between the physical world and that of spirit is at it's thinnest. It certainly seems that way for me as I've found that, every year, as October progresses I become more and more aware of the presence of spirit all around. All over the world at this time of year there are festivals to honour our loved ones and ancestors in spirit: The Pagan festival of Samhain, the Mexican Day of the Dead and many more. However, I don't think that it should be a melancholy time. They are reaching out and drawing close to us, and we can, if we choose, take this as a message that they are never far away and that we only need to think of and remember them in order to be close to them again. This is proven to me time and time again. You should take particular note of your dreams at this time of year.

The Tarot card 'Death' is traditionally associated with this time of year. However, this card is a very positive one, talking of new beginnings and the cycle of life. So, yes, think about those who have passed over, but then think about what they would want for us. Is it really that hard to believe that they would want us to be happy and get on with living our lives to the best that we possibly could?

You may feel that there are some things you would prefer to let go of, such as negative thoughts or habits, a situation at work or in your personal life. If you think that you may have some stuff to let go of, even if your heart doesn't want to, why not try the following?

- Write down what it is that you think you would like to be rid of.
- Make a list of reasons to get rid of it, then make a list of reasons to keep it. You may be misjudging what it is that you really want. Remember though, it is not the number of things on the list that counts, this is just a way of clarifying things for you, and one big reason could very well outweigh four or five smaller ones!
- Now ask yourself, "Do I want this thing to be a part of my life right now?"
- If the answer is now "yes", then that's fine. But you might want to reassess things again in a few months to be sure.
- If the answer is "no", then you will probably want to do something about it. Make a plan, it doesn't have to be anything huge, just one or two steps that will

get you on track to eliminating the thing you no longer want. Then gather up the lists you made and get rid of them - try shredding, tearing or burning (carefully). As you do, think about shedding the thing you no longer need in your life. Afterwards, have a cleansing shower or bath and let all thoughts of this 'thing' be washed away down the drain.

• Be positive and strive to make positive changes. Don't dwell on the 'giving up' or 'letting go'. And don't beat yourself up if you slip into old ways, just reassert your wish to let go of the 'thing' and take each day as it comes. Because each moment of your life is 'now', by focusing on doing something 'now' you practice doing it in each moment of your life.

If you do nothing else...

We are all spiritual beings but we do get caught up in the mechanics of living, working etc. That can't be helped and it's okay, but we do sometimes need reminding of 'who we are' don't we? Here are 3 simple things, which, if you do nothing else in the next 6 weeks, you should schedule into your life. Book time to be with the magical part of you and you will shine. So, if you do nothing else, between now and 21st of December,

1) Have some fun and carve a pumpkin. Light it up and watch it glow.

2) Arrange to spend some time with someone who makes you feel good, who you can laugh with. Maybe a friend or relative that you haven't seen for a while.

3) Put aside some time to spend on your own. Use it to take a look at the things you would really love to do or have in your life, but for some reason, won't or don't? This might be learning a new skill, moving home, changing jobs or taking the next step in developing your psychic skills. Ask yourself why you won't go there. Does it feel like too much hard work? Is it fear of failure? Is it just fear of going outside your comfort zone? Fear and excitement are very similar emotions, so why not turn fear around? Doing new things and accepting new challenges can take you to many new and exciting places and you will feel more fulfilled as a result. I once read that 'on the other side of comfort is adventure'. I can't remember where I read it, but it stuck with me and it's helped me to expand my experience of life. As you begin to live your life more fully you're expanding your comfort zone and will therefore do even more. Write some notes about your thoughts on this and we'll come back to them another time.

Go on then - put them in your diary now.

HAVE A COOL YULE
WINTER SOLSTICE, 20th-22nd December

The Solstice occurs between the 20th and 22nd of December and is the shortest day and longest night of the year. It was once a time to retreat and hibernate whilst waiting for the sun to bring new life in the spring. Nights will now gradually become shorter and the sun begins to return. In the depths of winter our ancestors believed that by affirming the life, light and energy of the sun, they would ensure it's return in order to begin the following agricultural cycle once more. Even in modern times these beliefs appear to be echoed with our use of bright decorations and lights at Midwinter / Christmas. It's worth remembering this almost primeval instinct to keep the light burning in times of darkness, especially when our own problems and those around the World appear to be overwhelming.

Now is a wonderful time of year to visit places of powerful earth energy such as ancient woodlands and even old churches decked out with holly, mistletoe and candles for Christmas.

Take some time to look inside and think about what it is that you would like to bring into your life, or nourish within yourself. What makes you come alive? When we shine with life and light, we enhance the lives of others and encourage and inspire them to improve themselves. In this way we all add to the lights shining around the world, dispelling the darkness.

Remember though, that we're all responsible for our own light. If it goes out, someone can help us to find a flame, offer their light to guide us, hand us a match to re-ignite it, even show us how to do it, but they can't re-light it for us or keep it lit in our behalf.

Ensure that all you do protects and strengthens your inner light and keeps it alive for you. Use it to get excited about your life, to get enthusiastic about the things that you do. This excitement and enthusiasm is like a forest fire - you can smell it, taste it and see it from a mile away, and it spreads to those around you.

"When you possess a light within you, you see it externally"

Anais Nin

If you do nothing else...

We are all spiritual beings but we do get caught up in the mechanics of living, working etc. That can't be helped and it's okay, but we do sometimes need reminding of 'who we are' don't we? Here are 3 simple things, which, if you do nothing else in the next 6 weeks, you should schedule into your life. Book time to be with the magical part of you and you will shine. So, if you do nothing else, between now and 1st February,

1) At Halloween I suggested that you take some time to think about and write down something that you would really love to do or have in your life. Look at this again and add to it, create some short, medium and long term goals that you would like to aim for and write a target date next to each one.

2) In a notebook or on a noticeboard or large sheet of paper (which you can frame later if you really want something to focus on) place pictures, words or images which represent each of your goals. Take time over this, make it as real as possible, look through magazines for pictures and create a collage of your favourites. This is your 'Dreamscape' Use it to allow your dreams to escape and be released into the universe to become reality.

3) Now take time to look at each goal. Break it down in to the necessary stages which would allow you to reach it. Then break each stage down further in to manageable chunks. Next to each stage write a date when you will do it. There you are, now you have a plan of how to achieve your goals.

Go on then - put them in your diary now.

BEGINNING AGAIN
IMBOLC, 1st-2nd February

The 1st or 2nd of February (depending on the source) is traditionally associated with the Celtic Goddess, Brigid. She, and this time of year, is associated with re-emergence and initiation. It is a festival of light. In the agricultural calendar, it is the time when the early lambs are being born, snowdrops are emerging through the still-hard ground and the days are getting longer. It's a lovely time of year to get out walking and observe the first signs of life as spring approaches. It's a time to celebrate everything feminine, visit ancient wells where the goddesses would have been worshipped and prayed to.

Do you feel as though a part of you has vanished or that something is missing? What within you is searching for the light? Is there a skill that needs nourishing? What needs to be swept away?

This is a time of creativity, innovation and new enterprise. It is also associated with inner wisdom, candle magic and meditation. If you have questions, doubts or feelings that you would like clarification on, meditation by candle light may be of benefit to you. Or try your hand at poetry. a brilliant way to look inside yourself and be creative at the same time. You don't have to let anyone else read it, it's just for you. Below is a verse from a poem that I wrote about this time of year.

"On the path, but lost and lonely
the cool sunlight will inspire.
Feel your soul, in the darkness,
drawn to the light of a candle's flame,
the winter's sleep cast off at last,
Your eyes are cleansed, you see again."

If you do nothing else...
We are all spiritual beings but we do get caught up in the mechanics of living, working etc. That can't be helped and it's okay, but we do sometimes need reminding of 'who we are' don't we? Here are 3 simple things, which, if you do nothing else in the next 6 weeks, you should schedule into your life. Book time to be with the magical part of you and you will shine. So, if you do nothing else, between now and 21st March,

1) Have a good old-fashioned spring clean. It doesn't have to be massive, maybe one room, or one cupboard, your wardrobe, or that box that you've been meaning to sort for ages. Throw open the windows and let the spring into your home. Breathe deeply and enjoy the fresh air. It's amazing how different it can make you feel.

2) Plant some seeds. If you think that you don't have room or time why not try one of my favourites, a chilli plant. They are so easy to grow, just use dried seeds from a shop bought chilli pepper. You will soon have a lovely little plant which in time will give you pretty little white flowers. Then the chillis will form which you can pick and cook with as and when you need them. They do need to be kept indoors, or in a greenhouse though.

3) Light a candle and meditate on it's flame for 15 - 20 minutes. Re-connect with your own inner light, and ask that you are able to sense that of others.

Go on then - put them in your diary now.

SPRING EQUINOX
OSTARA, 20th-22nd March

Between 20th and 22nd of March is the Spring Equinox. Traditionally this festival was named Ostara after the Germanic goddess of the fertile earth. It's not hard to see the origins of the word 'Easter' is it? Traditionally, both literally and symbolically, Easter is seen as a time of rebirth, spring flowers, lambs etc. Even when we've had snow at this time the flowers still manage to fight through. We give eggs at this time to represent these new beginnings. Let the spring energy inspire you and propel you forward to do the things you wish to do this year.

To me it feels like a time of transformation. It's as though the previous weeks, months, for some people, maybe even years have been a preparation phase during which time a chrysalis has been created, nurtured and cared for, and now is on the brink of a metamorphosis. A butterfly is about to break out of it's protective shell and emerge as a thing of beauty, taking flight, inspiring, enlightening and pioneering a new phase.

Assume for a moment that you are in that place, having absorbed all of your life experiences, feelings, opinions and knowledge to date. How would you emerge now? Where would your metamorphosis take you? What could you do with it? What would you wish to change in the world? What impact would you desire to leave on this planet? What small daily acts could you undertake to make this a reality for you and those around you right now?

Within your concept of these changes you can work on a small, local level, larger, national level or massively on a global scale. They are all valid ways, but they are not all practical. Instead of doing nothing, why not start small?

"You must be the change you wish to see in the world"
Ghandi

If you do nothing else...

We are all spiritual beings but we do get caught up in the mechanics of living, working etc. That can't be helped and it's okay, but we do sometimes need reminding of 'who we are' don't we? Here are 3 simple things, which, if you do nothing else in the next 6 weeks, you should schedule into your life. Book time to be with the magical part of you and you will shine. So, if you do nothing else, between now and 1st of May,

1) Get out into nature, even if it's just into the garden. Take some time to enjoy the sights, sounds and energy of your surroundings.

2) Give a little money to charity or buy a copy of the Big Issue - with love.

3) Take some time to think about what activities made you happy as a child, sports, drawing, acting, maybe just meeting up with friends. Write them down and then work out how you could re-introduce an element of them back into your life. This could mean taking up a new hobby or simply walking through mud in your wellies. Go out, have some fun, and laugh!

Go on then - put them in your diary now.

MAY DAY
BELTANE, 1st May

This festival was known by the ancient Celts as Beltane and marks the start of summer. It would have been celebrated from sunset on 30th of April and the festivities would have continued through the night, to watch the sunrise on the 1st of May. There are myths that tell of fairies coming out at this time looking for humans to lure to their lands. It's a fun and joyful time to celebrate the spiral of life and the pleasures of love.

Hawthorne blossom, also known as 'May' is symbolic of this season. The old saying, "N'er cast a clout 'til May be out" refers to the blossom rather than the month of May. However, traditionally it is said that you should not bring it into the house as this would invite the fairy folk in.

The Maypole that is danced around in English villages on May Day has many stories and associations. It's said by some to be a phallic representation of fertility and life. By others it's said to represent a garlanded tree, or the tree of life which bridges heaven and earth. Whatever it represents it's a focus for celebration, joy, fun and community. Take a day to enjoy a May festival near you.

Are you joyous? Are you happy with yourself just the way you are? Being kind to yourself as well as truly being yourself is essential. Beltane is a festival of light, life, love and fun. Embrace the start of summer, go out (or stay in!) and enjoy yourself. But look out for the fairy folk...

"Do anything, but let it produce joy"
Henry Miller

If you do nothing else...

We are all spiritual beings but we do get caught up in the mechanics of living, working etc. That can't be helped and it's okay, but we do sometimes need reminding of 'who we are' don't we? Here are 3 simple things, which, if you do nothing else in the next 6 weeks, you should schedule into your life. Book time to be with the magical part of you and you will shine. So, if you do nothing else, between now and 21st of June,

1) Treat yourself to some time off - maybe it's a couple of hours on your own doing things that you enjoy or doing nothing. Book a pamper day, a makeover, a meditation class or massage. Let yourself enjoy it and know that you are worth it.

2) Find out when the next full moon is and go out for a walk enjoying it's gentle glow.

3) Go and search out a book of a spiritual nature in a bookshop or library that you haven't yet read. If there isn't one that you've had in mind, let yourself be guided to one that you may benefit from reading.

Go on then - put them in your diary now.

MIDSUMMER
SUMMER SOLSTICE, 20th-22nd June

Midsummer is a great time. Day and night are equal, and the long summer evenings, hopefully warm enough for us to sit outside, are very welcome. But why is it always such a surprise that it can still be light at 10pm? It happens every year!

I love to visit standing stones at this time of year. Avebury in Wiltshire has the most wonderful stone circle which surrounds the entire village. At the Solstices and Equinoxes there are always wonderful Druidic Rituals within this massive stone circle and everyone is invited to observe and sometimes to join them. The local pub which is also inside the circle is definitely haunted, although I would question it's place as one of the top ten most haunted locations in the world!

The stones are *so* worth a visit. I absolutely love this place, spending time lazing around the stones, soaking up their energy, plus that of the earth, wind and sun. It's extremely relaxing and I think you need that time to really relax properly before you can truly recharge and set off again. A bit like completely running down a battery from time to time before recharging it. You will come back invigorated and ready for life again. And that is what midsummer is about, living your life.

This is a time of fulfillment, culmination, warmth, enjoyment and seizing the day. Celebrate the summer and yourself.

Remember also that we are a part of the creative force of the universe and we all weave our part of the web of life. We are connected with everything else and impact on others as much as they impact on us.

Be thankful for all that you have, for your friends and family, for your accomplishments and the lessons you have learnt in your journey so far.

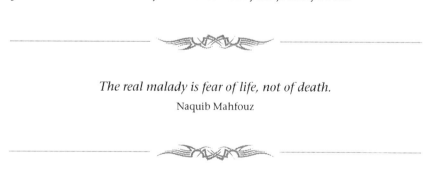

The real malady is fear of life, not of death.
Naquib Mahfouz

If you do nothing else...

We are all spiritual beings but we do get caught up in the mechanics of living, working etc. That can't be helped and it's okay, but we do sometimes need reminding of 'who we are' don't we? Here are 3 simple things, which, if you do nothing else in the next 6 weeks, you should schedule into your life. Book time to be with the magical part of you and you will shine. So, if you do nothing else, between now and 1st of August,

1) Plan a get together, party, BBQ or day out with people close to you. Play games, chat, laugh, eat and enjoy the company of others.

2) Attend a Summer fete or community event.

3) Pick or buy a beautiful bunch of flowers and place them somewhere that you will see them as much as possible.

Just get out there and enjoy it... go on then... put something in your diary now!

BRIGHT BLESSINGS

MY RAMBLINGS

WATCH FOR THE SIGNS

One morning I went to open the dining room curtains and there, sitting on a patio chair was a beautiful buzzard looking at me over it's shoulder. It made me feel great for the rest of the day. We get quite a few buzzards wher we live and often sit and watch them catching the thermals and circling higher and higher, but I never imagined one would come into the garden. I decided to look up the symbolism of the buzzard in one of my books but it wasn't listed. However, whilst flicking through I noticed a picture of some hawks that looked very similar to my buzzard. For the hawk, it read 'awakens our vision and inspires us to a creative life purpose'*.

Later, in the evening I was doing some writing and a little white spider came along and sat on some of my papers. It spent the whole evening with me, running over my notes or just sitting watching me type. As before, I looked in my book to see what symbolism a spider has and found, amongst other things, the following: 'Creativity and the weaving of fate. The spider awakens creative sensibilities. Spider reminds us that the world is woven around us. We are keepers and writers of our own destiny, weaving it like a web by our thoughts, feelings and actions.'* (*from Animal-Speak by Ted Andrews).

These two 'messages' seemed to go well together and were in keeping with the fact that I had spent the day writing and working on a book. I was also reminded of the words to the song 'Unwritten' by Natasha Beddingfield, that had been going around my head for a couple of weeks. I am unable to include them here due to copyright restrictions but I found them very thought provoking, and you may wish to listen to it.

My point is that the universe does speak to us, giving signs of encouragement and confirmation. We simply need to be open enough to see, acknowledge and embrace them.

We also write our own story, with our actions and our thoughts. We weave our own web and create our own destiny. Part of this involves how willing we are to learn, to truly see what goes on around us and to take responsibility. But part of it also involves our faith or belief in a connected Universe, or not. Whatever you believe in relation to this will determine how you see your own life and whether you believe you have control over it or not.

I prefer to believe that I can create my own destiny and tread my own path, and that the Universe truly wishes me to do that. It will therefore help me along the way and send me messages and signs confirming that what I am doing is right for me. However, everyone's path is different and must be congruent with what we truly feel inside, otherwise it will be too difficult a terrain for us to navigate.

3 Quotes About
'Messages'

"All major religious traditions carry basically the same message, that is love, compassion and forgiveness ... the important thing is they should be part of our daily lives."

Dalai Lama

"If the sight of the blue skies fills you with joy, if a blade of grass springing up in the fields has power to move you, if the simple things in nature have a message you understand, Rejoice, for your soul is alive."

Eleanora Duse

"A message prepared in the mind reaches a mind; a message prepared in a life reaches a life."

Bill Gothard

A LESSON LEARNT

I get extremely irate with people who park inconsiderately in our town, on double yellows or by double-parking, causing the main street to become blocked. One weekend we had friends staying with us and, on returning to the town after a day out, I could be heard being very unspiritual towards certain drivers who had committed these offences and clogged the street. The following day my friend and I popped out to the shops, we were chatting away when we were stopped by an elderly lady in the street. She asked us if we could possibly help her as she had extremely swollen and painful feet and felt that she couldn't walk another step. She only lived a few hundred yards away but wondered whether we could give her a lift, if we had a car. She was walking with a stick and her feet were indeed very swollen, one was badly bruised and the other bandaged. As I live in the town, my car was just around the corner so she waited in one of the shops where they kindly gave her a chair and my friend and I returned to get the car. When I drove towards the shop where we had left this lady I realised that there were no parking spaces and that the only way I could pick her up was to stop on the opposite side of the road - yes, on double yellow lines. My friend jumped out and helped the lady up from her chair, across the road and into the car. We drove to the end of the street and I turned the car around so that she didn't have to cross the road to get home. Lo and behold, once more there was absolutely nowhere to pull in, so guess what? My only option was to double-park in order that my friend could help this very grateful old lady out of the car. The irony of the day's events were not lost on me.

SO... I guess I need to remember that story the next time I get annoyed with someone without knowing all the facts. I'm sure there are those who do what they like without thinking of the consequences to others but on the other hand, they could well be doing someone a huge favour, and find doing that annoying thing to me a small price to pay. I hope that this experience makes me a nicer person, particularly towards other drivers - and so does my husband!

3 Quotes About
'Lessons'

*"Remember, there are no mistakes, only lessons.
Love yourself, trust your choices,
and everything is possible."*
Cherie Carter-Scott

*"One of the most important lessons that experience teaches
is that, on the whole, success depends more upon character
than upon either intellect or fortune"*
William Edward Hartpole Lecky

*"Courage allows the successful woman to fail and learn
powerful lessons from the failure so that in the end,
she didn't fail at all"*
Maya Angelou

THREE GIFTS FOR YOU

I have three gifts to pass on to you. Take some time to think about them and try to integrate some aspects of them into your life:

Firstly; 'Be You'
The more that you are, and express, who you really are, the more you will feel in the flow of life. It's a powerful thing to give yourself permission to be who you truly are - do it now. Once in the flow, things will fall into place and happen naturally, almost magically.

Secondly; 'You are Perfect'
In every moment you are perfect, given what you need to learn, experience, remember or act upon in that same moment. This doesn't mean that you have to stay the same forever. If you don't like certain aspects of yourself, acknowledge them, then seek ways to accept, alter or overcome them. Don't be too hard on yourself, the key point to remember is that, right now, you are perfect, given what you need to learn, experience, remember or act upon. So, what does this mean? In any moment your personal journey may require you to be or act in a particular way, therefore you may see a facet of yourself that allows you to be or do just that. You may not like this part of yourself, and that may be the whole point. You may then seek to alter that part of yourself. Therefore in the moment that you realised there was a part of you that you disliked, you chose to be or act in a different way in order to change it. As this was a part of your personal evolution, you were, in fact, perfect in that moment, for that required outcome. As, indeed, you are perfect in the next moment, and the next. You are perfect now. Think about it.

Thirdly; 'Life is Perfect'
This is sometimes a hard one to get your head around but bear with me. Every person, every moment and every circumstance is perfect given what you are to draw from them. See perfection in yourself, in others and in situations. It is difficult, it's about the bigger picture, but when things are tough, and when they're not, tell yourself that 'Life is Perfect'.

If you can take these on board in even the tiniest way, it's amazing how much easier life becomes - or maybe it just seems that way, whichever, the result is the same.

3 Quotes About
'Perfection'

*"Everything is perfect in the universe,
even your desire to improve it"*

Wayne Dyer

*"To improve is to change;
to be perfect is to change often"*

Winston Churchill

*"The true perfection of man lies not in
what a man has, but what a man is"*

Oscar Wilde

GETTING SOME ACTION

For many years I have known that one of my biggest 'faults' is procrastination. When it's necessary for me to study for an exam, it's amazing how essential to life the cleaning of the skirting boards becomes. And when faced with having to make a tricky call, or write an awkward letter; "I'll just have a cup of tea first and then I'll do it". I know that while my list-making can be essential, on occasion it's simply another way for me to procrastinate. On top of all that, my natural tendency is to do the easy stuff first. That way I feel that I have achieved more and my 'to do' list goes down more quickly. However, the feeling of accomplishment is soon overtaken by the sinking feeling when I realise that the job I have been putting off is still lurking around, waiting to be done. Procrastination is a quality which I have been striving to overcome for some time, and I am getting better. When I am being really good, I reverse my natural tendency and do the worst jobs first, and that makes me feel so much better. So what is the solution? Quite simply, take action.

This message of 'Action' has been thrown at me from everywhere in the last four weeks, seminars, friends, readings, books and my own thoughts and realisations. I think it applies to so much more than my dislike for doing the hard stuff. Now I have chosen to ask myself, 'Take action or make excuses - which is more productive?'.

In my experience, we all achieve so much more when we are 'walking the walk', we feel more in tune with life and things fall into place. The key is that what you say and do must be in harmony.

If Thoughts = Dreams, and Action = Results, then Thoughts+Action = Realisation of your Dreams. That's a powerful equation.

I will often have an idea and create a plan, then sit waiting for some motivation, inspiration, sign, energy (or caffeine fix!) to get me started. What I actually need to do to get started, is to START! It's not rocket science is it?

So, what are you waiting for?

3 Quotes About
'Action'

"It's important to know that words
don't move mountains.
Work, exacting work, moves mountains"

Danilo Dolci

"Nobody made a greater mistake than he who
did nothing because he could only do little."

Edmund Burke

"First say to yourself what you would be;
and then do what you have to do"

Epictetus

INNER STILLNESS

Even when my life is crazy, I am fortunate enough that the 'Powers that Be' intersperse my 'work stuff' with meeting amazing, like-minded people, spiritual encounters and a constant stream of messages, coincidences and confirmations for me about all aspects of my life. Now, some of you might consider me lucky for this to be the case, but I believe that these things are available to everyone.

If you want to have a more spiritual and connected life, simply decide that you will. Ask for it and expect it. Open your mind, your eyes and your heart. Look for the soul in the eyes of each person that you encounter, even if they are just passing you in the street, and listen to the messages that others bring you. Life is busy but if we have an inner stillness we will experience the spirituality and connection of every moment. And the more experiences we have, the more experiences we will have. That might sound odd at first but it *is* true, because with each experience our belief is confirmed and then we can trust more.

Be still and know.

*"Within you there is a stillness and a sanctuary to which you
can retreat at any time."*
Hermann Hesse

3 Quotes About
'Happiness'

"Happiness comes when your work and words
are of benefit to yourself and others"
Buddha

"The best remedy for those who are afraid, lonely or
unhappy is to go outside, somewhere where they can be
quiet, alone with the heavens, nature and God.
Because only then does one feel that all is as it should be
and that God wishes to see people happy,
amidst the simple beauty of nature."
Anne Frank

"Happiness is when what you think, what you say
and what you do are in harmony"
Mohandas Gandhi

SEEKING BALANCE

Here is a lesson that we all know in theory but how often do we put it into practice? In amongst all the 'work' stuff, 'home' stuff, 'keeping everyone fed, watered and happy' stuff, what do you do for you?

Life will always seek balance. And we need to do this too. One particularly busy week I had a mountain of paperwork to do, three 7a.m. breakfast meetings, two evening meetings as well as daytime appointments and a newsletter to write. My meetings generally take between 30 and 50 minutes to drive to and from, and I was in desperate need for a massage as my shoulders were killing me. But I also chose to spend time chatting and laughing with a friend over dinner one night and two evenings at dance classes as we were rehearsing for a public performance. By the Friday I wasn't sure if I could stay awake a moment longer. However, on the Saturday we did our performances in Shrewsbury town centre, the sun came out for us, and we didn't make too many mistakes! Friends and family came to watch, everyone loved it and we got a real buzz from it. It was so worth taking the time to practice and take part in something that I really enjoy, it keeps me energised and smiling and it makes thoughts of work vanish so that I remember what life is really about.

So my thought here is to take some time to do something for yourself that makes you smile. Spend time with a friend, dance, sing, go for a walk, make chicken soup, whatever you enjoy, and don't apologise to anyone for it. For once, why not be a bit selfish - I believe that it will make you a better person!

"I enjoyed my own nature to the fullest, and we all know that there lies happiness, although, to soothe one another mutually, we occasionally pretend to condemn such joys as selfishness."

Albert Camus, French philosopher and Writer. Nobel prize winner

3 Quotes About
'Balance'

"Life is like riding a bicycle. To keep your balance, you must keep moving"
Albert Einstein

"Be aware of wonder. Live a balanced life - learn some and think some and draw and paint and sing and dance and play and work every day some"
Robert Fulghum

"Problems arise in that one has to find a balance between what people need from you and what you need for yourself"
Jessye Norman

TAKE CONTROL OF YOUR TIME

I know that when I take time to sit and meditate, attend a course or class, or allow myself the time to read a book without worrying about other things, I come away from the experience, not only with a more positive outlook but feeling fulfilled and ready to get on and do the next thing.

I also know that if I have 101 things to do, don't prioritise, procrastinate and dip in and out of things, I get stressed and nothing gets done.

So I have been experimenting with my time management skills in the last two or three weeks, and it has been really useful. I've got loads more done and I have been really focussed on the things that I have undertaken.

One of the things I have been doing is to schedule the things from my 'To Do' list into my diary, this way they are far more likely to get done. I have given myself permission to forget about all the other stuff that needs doing - because they are scheduled into be looked at later in the week. This means that I can really concentrate on what I am doing in that moment.

I used to think that if someone else suggested an appointment time or a specific day for an activity, I might miss an opportunity so I would say yes and then have to rearrange my plans, or simply put other jobs or my own activities off. I now know that I can have more control by saying that 'I have plans on that day, but what about the Tuesday or Thursday?'. And guess what? Those 'others' don't actually mind, because they know what it's like to be busy too.

This may seem obvious, but I think it's easy to overlook the obvious. Since starting this exercise I have felt a much greater sense of achievement and am feeling far more organised. All I needed was a bigger diary to write everything down in. Plus I feel that this is only the beginning, I'm not quite there yet, wherever 'there' is, but things can only improve.

"The first rule of focus is this: 'Wherever you are, be there'."

Author unknown

3 Quotes About
'Time'

*"For every minute spent organising,
an hour is earned"*

Author Unkown

*"How we spend our days is, of course,
how we spend our lives"*

Annie Dillard

*"Time is free, but it's priceless.
You can't own it but you can use it.
You can't keep it, but you can spend it.
Once you've lost it you can never get it back."*

Harvey Mackay

GET IN THE FLOW

How do you know when you are on the right path? Spiritual people often talk of their life's purpose, being on the right path or feeling 'in the flow'. I have used all of these phrases myself but maybe some of you haven't. Maybe some of you have wondered what your life's purpose is, and how do you know what it feels like when you are doing it? Are we meant to know? Surely if everything happens for a reason, whatever we are doing is our life's purpose?

Personally I think that some people worry too much about this. Maybe instead of asking these sorts of questions we need to ask, Am I happy? Am I happy with my achievements so far? Am I happy with the changes I have made to my life? Am I happy with the goals I have set for myself? Am I happy having no goals but responding to the different events that occur as they happen? Am I happy with the way that I act and respond to these events, or to the people in my life? If any of these questions throw out an awkward feeling or a negative answer, what can you do to address that? How can you change it? How can you turn things around so that you do feel happier?

How do you know when you are 'on the right path? Sometimes I find that I simply feel very content and happy. At other times I find that it makes me feel quite neutral. I know that is a strange phrase to use but it's the only one I can think of to describe it. I feel guided, almost on autopilot, an observer of my own life often with no extreme of emotions (although this is kind of rare to be honest with you). There is a strange sense of 'being at home' even if seemingly odd or 'bad' things are happening. Somehow I just know that when I am doing what I am meant to be doing, everything falls into place and just happens. That doesn't mean that only 'good' things are going on. Even when 'bad' things happen, if you are 'in the flow' your responses are as you would wish them to be and they cause the correct chain of events to occur for the desired outcome. This can come as a surprise to you, even if you feel that you are used to being 'in the flow'.

So, how do you get 'in the flow' or on the right path? Start by being yourself, taking time for you, discover what makes you happy, think about where you want to be and how you would like to get there. Maybe it's time to start something new. Taking action and therefore taking control helps you to feel more 'in the flow', then you *are* more 'in the flow'. I also find that smiling helps.

3 Quotes About
'Life Purpose'

"Look and you will find it ~ what is unsought
will go undetected."

Sophocles

"You are a child of the Universe, no less than the moon
and the stars; you have a right to be here.
And whether or not it is clear to you,
no doubt the Universe is unfolding as it should."

Max Ehrmann

"The purpose of life is to live a life of purpose"

Richard Leider

BEING YOURSELF, ALL THE TIME

My life has changed, I have learnt to really integrate my spiritual side into my every-day stuff. It's allowed me to meet so many amazing people who are also very spiritual and make connections by actually being brave enough to talk about my beliefs to people. I am not suggesting everyone should enter into philosophical debates with every person they meet, but personally I am not as worried as I used to be about telling people about myself. I go with my instinct though, sometimes you just know not to mention it to certain people. You also learn about what sort of language to use too. I don't recommend, 'Hello, I'm Psychic' or, for some of you, 'Hiya, I think I'm a witch', or, as my brother-in-law likes to joke with me about, 'I see dead people'. These intros don't really go down too well - can't think why? I guess what I have found out in recent years is that you don't have to compartmentalise your life into 'work', 'home', 'family', 'spiritual practices' etc. Let them mix, be you, and who you are includes all of those things. Why not test the waters by asking others if they have had any of the spiritual experiences that you have had? You don't have to put yourself on the line with this one, maybe mention that someone you know was talking about 'this thing' the other day and ask them what they think about it. People always have an opinion. The more you talk about your beliefs the more you work out what they are.

Warning: Take this easy, one small step at a time, I have spent a long time working out my beliefs and getting to a point where I can discuss them using the right language that won't fire people up the wrong way. A great starting point if you want to discuss matters of a psychic nature is to bring up the subject of ghost stories, most people have one and are fascinated by them, it can lead on to all sorts of topics and if you discover that someone is not of a similar mindset to you, you can laugh it off as a bunch of silly stories.

Alternatively, start a discussion with yourself, in your head or on paper and see what you draw from it.

"We are so accustomed to disguise ourselves to others that in the end we become disguised to ourselves."

Francois Duc de La Rochefoucauld

3 Quotes About

'Laughter'

*"You don't stop laughing because you grow old.
You grow old because you stop laughing."*

Michael Pritchard

*"When people are laughing, they're generally not
killing one another."*

Alan Alda

"Laughter is inner jogging."

Norma Cousins

TELLING TALES

We all love telling ghost stories from time to time, don't we? Mind you, mine just aren't that scary. Contrary to popular, media-led opinion, paranormal encounters aren't usually that scary. As a child, when I saw spirit walking through our family home, I often didn't even mention it. Although, waking up to see spirit standing in your home in the middle of the night was not always so pleasant as both my sisters will attest to. As we get older our brains get bombarded with Hollywood imagery and fuelled by teenage urban myths causing our minds to associate spirit activity with something really scary and dangerous. As a result, alot of us put barriers up which can stunt our personal, spiritual and psychic development.

I am not going to suggest that you all go and seek out hauntings and troubled souls without training and knowledge in this area or without a good, trustworthy team to back you up. But I would like to give you a few hints and tips which may help to allay any fears that you have and perhaps encourage you to open your mind to further development.

There are two types of 'haunting'. The first are caused by residual energy. This is like a residue or recording of an event in the fabric of a place or building. It would be much like someone projecting a film on to a screen. While this may be a bit odd at first, it's not going to cause you any harm. The second type of haunting is as a result of an earthbound spirit who has, for whatever reason, not moved on to the spiritual realm. The thing to remember here is that they are in our physical world and it takes a lot of energy for spirit to manifest or to cause physical activity, so we are stronger. One way that they gain strength is to use our fearful energy, so the best thing is not to let them have it. Keep your mood upbeat and positive. I always encourage a sense of humour as laughter can really help to battle fear and will discourage any negative entities.

I have never liked the term 'supernatural' and have always said that if it happens, which it does, it must be natural. As with anything in life, there is always going to be an element of risk, fear, or doubt. However, it is important to remember that in the majority of cases, when an event is encountered it's usually met with a sense of acceptance. To illustrate this point I would like to tell one of my ghost stories, so if you are sitting comfortably, then I'll begin.

Some years ago, my husband, John and I worked in London. This particular evening we had to get the train home instead of driving. We had a 15-20 minute walk to the nearest mainline station and it was a nice Autumnal evening around dusk. We walked away from the busy shops and restaurants of Bayswater and into a more residential area. Our journey took us through an alleyway which ran between two end-terrace houses with walled back gardens. As we turned into this alleyway we could see a lady carrying large heavy bags walking up towards us. We continued talking as we walked and finally emerged in the next street. As we did so, we both stopped and turned to each other, looking a little bemused we both commented that the lady hadn't passed us. We looked back, then up and down the street but there was no sign of her. Although neither of us had seen it, we both felt that she had turned off to our right, so, in order to satisfy our curiousity we walked back down the alley to see if there was an entrance into one of the gardens. Sure enough, in the wall, on that side of the alley, there was an arched entrance into a garden. However, it was bricked up! I am fairly used to seeing and sensing 'strange' things, this was my kind of 'normal'. But I was pleasantly surprised when John just said, "So things like that do happen then".

3 Quotes About
'*Fear*'

"Death is not the biggest fear we have;
our biggest fear is taking the risk to be alive —
the risk to be alive and express what we really are."

Don Miguel Ruiz

"Let us not look back in anger or forward in fear,
but around in awareness."

James Thurber

"And as we let our own light shine, we unconsciously give
other people permission to do the same. As we are liberated
from our fear, our presence automatically liberates others."

Marianne Williamson

PLAN TO EXPAND

Life is an amazing journey, there is so much to see, learn, do and experience. Don't give yourself a hard time if you feel that you haven't done as much as you would have liked so far? There are many ways that you can achieve more.

Why don't you plan to expand? No, I don't mean your waistline, your horizons, your mindset, your knowledge. Whatever you wish to expand, here's where you can start. Would you like to know more, understand more, achieve more, have more, be more this time next year? Well why not plan to do just that?

When John and I learnt to dive (a massive challenge for me as I was terrified of being in the sea!) one of the lessons was, 'Plan your Dive and Dive your Plan'. With your buddy you plan exactly what you are going to do during your dive, you also make a contingency plan in case circumstances change, and then you stick to it. This way you know where you're going and what you're doing, you achieve your goals, it makes you safer, and there is flexibility if things change. If you simply float along, you don't see or achieve as much as you could, you will probably get bored and if circumstances change, you may panic.

So why not take time to plan to do something different; take a class, read that book, take up a challenge, meet more people, try a new sport, meditate regularly, get out into nature, write a diary. Be specific, quantify it and set some dates for achieving it. Plan to live, then live your plan. I think you will achieve more and find more wonderful opportunities than ever before. But as always, it's up to you to actually go out there and do it. Go on then, what are you waiting for?

"Then indecision brings it's own delays
And days are lost lamenting o'er lost days
Are you in earnest? Seize this very minute
Whatever you do, or dream you can, begin it
Boldness has genius and power and magic in it."
Johann Wolfgang von Goethe

3 Quotes About
'Ideas'

"An idea is salvation by imagination"
Frank lloyd Wright

"Man's mind, once stretched by a new idea,
never regains its original dimensions."
Oliver Wendell Holmes

"Do something, if it doesn't work,
do something else. No idea is too crazy"
Jim Hightower

MAGICAL MANIFESTATION

When John and I decided to move to the country, we wrote a list of all the things we wanted of a location - and we found them. We also wrote a list of all the qualities we wanted in our new home. We were so sure that it was the right thing for us to do that we simply knew it would work out perfectly. And it did. Everything fell into place perfectly and when I looked at our wish list later I could tick off everything on it as having been received - with much thanks.

I, and people who I have worked with in development groups, have had so many experiences of manifestation. It can be used for anything from getting a new job, to finding the right car and even getting that elusive parking space. With simple things like the parking space, it's pretty easy to use visualisation techniques on their own but with manifesting the bigger stuff, there are three key elements in getting what you want:

1) Write it down and be specific
2) Believe and know that you will receive
3) Be thankful for receiving it, even before you physically have it

A great tool is a 'gratitude' or 'blessings' book. You can write in it all of the things that you are grateful for as well as anything that you wish to attain as though you already have it. This states to the Universe that you know it already exists for you and that you are thankful. By the law of attraction it will then find its way to you.

Please don't use this as an excuse for doing nothing however. Make a plan to achieve the situation or item you desire and start to work towards it, this activity combined with belief, thanks and the law of attraction will cause magical manifesation to work for you.

I was talking to a lady who works with a charity called 'The Hunger Project'. They don't throw money and food at those in the third world who are starving but effect positive change, helping them to help themselves. Those they help become independent, and have found their own solutions, committing themselves to taking action, however small. And I asked her if she ever noticed that as these projects progress, things just seemed to happen, almost by magic. 'Oh yes' she told me, which, of course, I knew she would!

3 Quotes About

'Mysteries'

"The final mystery is oneself"

Oscar Wilde

"Without mysteries, life would be very dull indeed. What would be left to strive for if everything were known?"

Charles de Lint

"Mystery is at the heart of creativity. That, and surprise."

Julia Cameron

TRUST IN YOU

As I write this, the birds are singing and remnants of the sunlight is shining on the tops of the hills. Ancient cultures performed rituals and ceremonies to ensure that the sun would return after the winter, or even the next morning. We don't seem so concerned with that now. Hasn't the sun come up every morning for all of our lives, no matter what else has been going on? Haven't we got more important things to worry about? We know that it's going to come up, don't we? To be truthful, we don't even give it any consideration. We trust that the sun will reappear each day, without question.

In life, stuff happens! When we are in it, it can be so hard to get out and move on. Yet a lot of ancient spiritual philosophy talks of rising above earthly concerns and emotions so that we observe and learn but do not experience or become affected by them - that aint gonna happen in a hurry is it?

However, if you have a strong sense of trust, whether that be in yourself, God, Goddess, The Universe, A.N.Other God, some sort of faith, it really does help you through those moments.

If you find it difficult to keep the faith when facing life's trials, try starting with something small, keep telling yourself, "The sun will come up tomorrow".

"If we had no winter, the spring would not be so pleasant; if we did not sometimes taste of adversity, prosperity would not be so welcome."
Anne Bradstreet

3 Quotes About
'Sunshine'

"Just living is not enough. One must have sunshine, freedom and a little flower."

Hans Christian Andersen

"Anyone who says sunshine brings happiness has never danced in the rain"

unknown

"Those who bring sunshine to the lives of others cannot keep it from themselves."

James Matthew Barrie

ENVIRONMENTALLY FRIENDLY?

Is the climate changing? Are we negatively impacting the environment? Can we really make a difference by making small changes in our everyday lives? Or is it completely beyond our control?

For me, and I am sure, others who have a more spiritual way of thinking. This debate also raises many other issues to contemplate.

Are we living our lives in keeping with our spiritual beliefs?

What impact do we have on those around us?

How do we want to be remembered when we end this existence?

For some, caring about our environment is intricately linked with their spiritual beliefs. Others don't consider one to have anything to do with the other. For me, respect for the earth, the cycles of nature and the huge energy system that is our universe, and that we are all a part of, is essential.

But it's not just the environment we affect. We impact upon all those who we cross paths with, however fleetingly. How do you affect those around you and those you pass in the street? How do others see you? Try smiling at the next stranger you pass and put it to the test. They will either smile back, or look confused - only because they are not used to it, either way, you have affected them.

I have always felt that life should be a bit like having a picnic, we should leave the area as we found it. But if we can leave it a slightly nicer place, so much the better.

So, some metaphorical self analysis...

Do you take all your rubbish home? And do you pick up after others and take that too?

Point to contemplate: If we are all one, and interconnected, what we do to each other and how we affect the natural world, we do to ourselves.

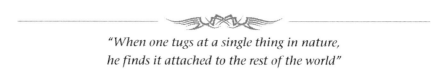

"When one tugs at a single thing in nature,
he finds it attached to the rest of the world"

John Muir

3 Quotes About
'Change'

"They say that time changes things, but actually you have to change them yourself"

Andy Warhol

"The important thing is this: to be able at any moment, to sacrifice what we are for what we could become."

Charles Dubois

"Unless you change how are you, you will always have what you've got"

Jim Rohn

GET PASSIONATE

After a great Christmas and New Year break at the end of 2007 I went to see my cousin, Jane, in Ireland for a few days. I had felt a bit lost in the last couple of months of the year and needed some time to find my path again and Jane, as well as having a very similar life view as me, is a life coach. We spent 5 days talking, drinking tea and eating scones, looking out over the wild Irish coastline, enjoying a log fire and good wine in the evening and making plans. It was great, relaxing, enlightening and inspiring. I came home with a much clearer vision of my life's purpose and with renewed drive and self-understanding. Taking a five day break for yourself may not always be possible, but even just taking half a day to focus on what you want to do and how you are going to do it, perhaps talking it over with a friend, or just with yourself, is something that, I believe, everyone should do once in a while.

Something that we discussed during this time was finding a passion.

Do you have a real passion for the things that you do? If not, try to find something you get excited about doing, something that you will feel proud of achieving. Where could that take you? What impact could that have on your life and on others? Think about it, is there something that you feel strongly about changing in your life, your community, your country, the world? How could you use your skills to go about making those changes? It doesn't have to be your full time occupation but it could be something that you work on a little at a time. Would it make your life more fulfilling?

The way you feel about something comes across in the way that you speak about it. It can't be helped. You know when someone is passionate about a subject, it's almost contagious.

I love to introduce people to a more spiritual way of thinking, I like to make them think more. I want to encourage an open-minded approach to life and non-judgemental attitude to others. I want to help each of you to enhance your energy vibration and leave a more positive impact on all of those that you come into contact with. You can do that with a simple smile. Learning to be content with the world, finding your path, being the best person that you can be at any given moment in time. That's what I am passionate about and that's what I want to share with you. What do you want to do?

3 Quotes About
'*Passion*'

"The most powerful weapon on earth is the human soul on fire."
Field Marshal Ferdinand Foch

"Anyone can dabble, but once you've made that commitment, your blood has that particular thing in it, and it's very hard for people to stop you."
Bill Cosby, Comedian

"The future may be made up of many factors but where it truly lies is in the hearts and minds of men.
Your dedication should not be confined for your own gain, but unleashes your passion for our beloved country as well as for the integrity and humanity of mankind."
Li Ka Shing, Chinese Businessman

MAKING A DIFFERENCE

Following a 5k 'Race For Life' that I ran with my two sisters, I enrolled in The Great North Run, half marathon. 'Why?' was a common question asked when I told people. Well, what better way to get fit, celebrate being alive and help others? It was summed up in a message I read on the back of one lady's top taking part in the 'Race For Life', "I run for those who can't, because I can"

What could you do that would make a difference in your life, and in others'?

I believe that the key to making a difference is taking part in, instigating something, or effecting a change that affects you in a positive way as well as others. There are many people who subjugate their selves for other people. And whilst that may appear to help some, whom does it truly serve? Does it set a good example to observers? It certainly doesn't help those doing the sacrificing. Many times, those on the receiving end are more dependent as a result. If we all made small changes or took some tiny action that benefited ourselves and one other person, place or thing, it would be a win-win situation and we would all feel great. Charity work can have a 'feel good' factor of its own, but what about in everyday life? Haven't we all, at some point been guilty of putting others before ourselves time and time again. Often with negative effect as we wear ourselves out, feel put upon, wonder if we will ever have time for ourselves again or even, wonder who we really are in amongst all the 'doing things for other people'?

Maybe it's time to ask yourself what would you like to achieve in your life that would make *you* smile? When we are happy in ourselves we are of much more use to others. We bring a positive energy to the proceedings, we rise above everything and we get so much more done. When we are down, or low, we drag our heels, pull others down with us and don't really achieve much. So by being kind to ourselves we will actually be able to help others more effectively. Let's get a bit of, well, not selfishness, I once heard it described as 'enlightened self interest'. Let's do that. And then, as we are happy with who we are, we can effect positive change in others and magic will happen. Believe me, I know it will.

3 Quotes About
'Making a Difference'

"It's easy to make a buck. It's a lot tougher to make a difference."

Tom Brokaw

"Never be afraid to do something new. Remember, amateurs built the ark; professionals built the Titanic."

Anonymous

"We must not, in trying to think about how we can make a big difference, ignore the small daily differences we can make which, over time, add up to big differences that we often cannot foresee."

Marian Wright Edelman

YOU ARE WHAT YOU SAY YOU ARE

I don't buy a newspaper, I find them too negative, plus I don't believe half the stuff they put in them. There is a saying that there are three sides a story, yours, mine and the truth. You could add a fourth, the version told by a journalist in order to sell more papers!

Am I being cynical? I don't know. I do watch the news to try and keep up to date with the world and I have been observing the media hype surrounding the current economic issues in the UK. I have attempted to observe the situation from a detached viewpoint and can't help thinking that alot of people are going to be either panicking or burying their heads in the sand.

Lets look at it from a more spiritual viewpoint:

Firstly it appears to demonstrate the law of attraction in a massive and quite detrimental way. The media have been determined to tell us how bad things are. Had there not been so much hype, would it be so bad? Have we helped to create an economic crisis by giving it so much of our attention as a nation? The law of attraction states that what we give out we get back. In 'The Secret' and similar books we are told that what we focus on becomes reality. I know that it works for positive thoughts therefore the reverse must also be true.

Secondly, maybe the situation will make us reflect on what we truly need in life compared to what we think we need. Do the trappings of modern living cause so much clutter that we cannot see the reality of it all? Do they feed the illusion that we are only physical beings? Can we get things back to the bare essentials and see who we really are and how we are connected to life?

And finally, can we use it to release our creativity? Historically human beings have been very inventive in times of lack. Now I know we are not at war or anything so awful but if you feel you need, or want to cut back, you will probably seek a creative work-around. These can be fun, far more social, and you may discover a new talent that you didn't know you had.

Lets think about steps we can take to make positive change in our lives now.

1) Attract things to you - Ask the universe to send you a coin in the next week - I bet you find one in the street or under the sofa or somewhere.

2) FREE time -Instead of spending money on a day out, go and do something free. Make a picnic and go for a walk. Greet people that you meet with a smile and, if you're really brave you could even try talking to them.

3) Start creating - Take one thing that you ordinarily buy ready-made, a cake, some pasta sauce, bread, a birthday card, whatever you can think of. Then make it yourself. Go on, it's fun. Or instead of watching TV why not paint a picture, play charades write a story or a piece of poetry. Take some cuttings from plants instead of buying new ones.

Some of these things may appear not very spiritual, perhaps a little mundane and practical but think about it: Focus on the positive, look at what is truly essential and important in your life and be creative. These will all help you to connect to who you really are, and that is a creative, spiritual being. Most importantly, enjoy it and have some fun!

3 Quotes About
'Reality'

"Reality is the only word in the English language that should always be used in quotes"

unknown

"There are some people who live in a dream world, and there are some who face reality; and then there are those who turn one into the other."

Douglas H. Everett

"The permanent temptation of life is to confuse dreams with reality. The permanent defeat of life comes when dreams are surrendered to reality."

Unknown

THE FULL MOON

One of the most beautiful, evocative and spiritual symbols, for me, is a full moon. It's an image so rich in myth, legend and symbolic association that I believe every person can relate to it in some way. What does it mean to you?

My husband, John says that his dad used to expect trouble on 'full moon' shifts when he was in the police. And my mum, when working on shifts in the social care sector would have the full moon marked up on the rotas as it would always coincide with one incident or another. Lunatics, Werewolves etc. there are so many negative associations.

It's said that when women live away from unnatural light (especially in tribal communities) their menstrual cycles are related with those of the moon. It also affects the ocean's tides. You can see its affect on our language through words such as 'lunatic' and 'month'. I, and others, have noticed increased business as the moon grows to full, whilst it falls off afterwards. I have also noticed that I dream more, or recall dreams more at a full moon. It's fascinating to take notice of the moon's cycles and how they coincide with life events, moods, activity levels etc. Why not try keeping a moon diary to see how it works for you? I wouldn't do this in order to deny or shift responsibility, but to observe, acknowledge and help you to go with the flow of life.

What does it mean to me? When I look up and see the beautiful orb of a full moon suspended against the night sky it makes me stop in my tracks. Everything else seems to fall away into insignificance. It relaxes me and it makes me smile and feel completely content. It gives me a sense of wonder and awe. It makes me feel complete and it immediately reminds me of my connection to Spirit.

Maybe the power of a full moon is simply that it reminds us that we are, without doubt, part of a bigger picture, and that we all play our part in life, no matter how insignificant we might think we are.

"May you have warm words on a cold evening, a full moon on a dark night and a smooth road all the way to your door."
Irish Blessing

3 Quotes About
'The Moon'

"When I admire the wonder of a sunset or the beauty of the moon, my soul expands in worship of the Creator."

Mahatma Gandhi

"See how nature - trees, flowers, grass - grows in silence; see the stars, the moon and the sun, how they move in silence... we need silence to be able to touch souls."

Mother Teresa

"Three things cannot be long hidden: the sun, the moon, and the truth"

Buddha

BOOK & PRODUCT REVIEWS

THE 'CONVERSATIONS WITH GOD' SERIES
BY NEALE DONALD-WALSCH

I have to admit that it took a while for me to get round to reading the first in the series of these books. I eventually had so many 'coincidences' relating to it that I knew I absolutely had to read it. Since then I have recommended these books to many people. They continue to be relative, profound and potentially life changing. I would highly recommend anyone who hasn't read them to give at least the first one a go. Please don't be put off by the use of the word 'God', I always say, see it as god with a small 'g' if it bothers you.

There are three initial 'Conversations with God' books, followed by 'Friendship with God',' Communion With God', 'The New Revelations', 'Tomorrow's God' and 'What God Wants'. I am half way through 'Tomorrow's God' and although they can be quite hard to get your head round, they are well worth the effort.

I am not usually one for a series of books such as these as they do tend to scream, 'here's a great big band wagon, lets get on it and ride it for all it's worth'. However, every one of these has resonated profoundly with me, and although I haven't got to the latest one in my collection, 'What God Wants', I have it on good authority, from a close friend, that it's also fantastic.

If these books are what they claim to be i.e. contact from God via automatic writing, it's amazing. If they're not, they are still inspired and inspiring (and one may ask, where has that inspiration come from in the first place?). As with any books in this genre, take from them what resonates with you. However, I would go out on a limb and say that the majority of you would find the information in them to be quite mind blowing - but in a good way! They are also very humorous, one friend came back to me after reading the first book and said, "Hasn't God got a great sense of humour?"

I think that I probably relate to something from these writings on an almost daily basis and I do not think that it would be too outrageous for me to say that these writings have truly empowered me and given me a new perspective on the meaning of life. (I've just re-read that last sentence and realised how amazing it sounds!)

"There's nothing you have to do, but there's a great deal you can be."
Neale Donald-Walsch, 'Conversations With God, Book 3'

'ANGEL NUMBERS'
BY DOREEN VIRTUE AND LYNNETTE BROWN

This isn't exactly a reading book but it's a great one to have in your collection. If you believe in 'meaningful coincidences' this is a great source of information to help interpret one way in which messages can come to you - through numbers.

Do you ever see certain numbers or number sequences over and over again? Do you wake up at night for no apparent reason, check the time and go back to sleep? Maybe the 'Powers That Be' are trying to tell you something through numbers. And if you don't believe in 'signs', you may find that this little book changes your mind. I can't tell you the number of times that I have looked a number up, only to find the most apt message. It's almost as if someone had planned it!

This book is good fun, if nothing else. You can get people to choose a number and then read out their message, or take the numbers from their birth date, car registration plate, house number etc.

The introduction helps you to understand how to use the book, especially for bigger numbers, then the numbers and their interpretations are listed from 00 to 999.

The RRP of this book is £4.99. Incidentally, 499's message is:

"The Angels say 'Get to work on your life mission now, without delay! Your purpose is much needed in the world.' If you're unsure what your purpose is, or what steps to take toward it, call upon and listen to the angels."

'JONATHAN LIVINGSTONE SEAGULL'
BY RICHARD BACH

An old'un, but a good'un. If you haven't read it, you should and if you read it a while back, I recommend re-visiting it. A short, easy, inspirational story that you can take as much or as little as you like from. On the back of the book it's described as, 'a story for people who follow their dreams and make their own rules; a story that has inspired people for decades'. I'm not going to say anymore, find out for yourself and see what happens!

'Richard Bach with this book does two things.
He gives me flight. He makes me Young.
For both I am deeply grateful.'
Ray Bradbury

'ONE MINUTE FOR YOURSELF - A SIMPLE STRATEGY FOR A BETTER LIFE'
BY SPENCER JOHNSON

Written as a modern day parable this little book is very powerful. It only takes a couple of hours to read but is full of simple wisdom to help you become more content and relaxed with life.

Starting with the simple philosophy of taking a minute, whenever you remember, to ask yourself, "Is there a way right now for me to take better care of myself?" The author then goes on to describe the phenomena that occur as a result of taking better care of yourself... you take better care of others. He tries to explain how it works, but even if you can't grasp the how or why, it's worth a shot just to see if it does. Personally, I think it will and I intend to start taking that one minute for myself from now on.

"'One minute isn't very long," the man complained.
"It's long enough to become happier." the older man said.
from 'One Minute For Yourself' by Spencer Johnson

'STEPPING INTO THE MAGIC: A NEW APPROACH TO EVERYDAY LIFE'
BY GILL EDWARDS

For me, this is most definitely a handbook for modern spiritual living. It covers subjects such as 'growth through joy', harmonising all aspects of yourself, abundance & manifestation, psychic development and fulfilling your true potential.

I think it's a great book for everyone. For beginners it touches on many different aspects of personal, spiritual and psychic development, giving enough information so as to inform and inspire, but not so much as to blow your mind. It will start you off on your path, leaving you the choice to pursue whichever of the more advanced subjects you are drawn to. For non-beginners, this book re-visits the basics as well as the more advanced subject matter with a down-to-earth, inspiring but practical approach. There are easy to follow exercises to get you started straight away, alongside material that you may wish to come back to at a later date. All in all, I believe this is a must-have book. You could use and re-use it in your development, possibly for years to come.

"There are only two differences between 'psychics' and the rest of us: first, psychics devote time to practicing their skills; and second, they trust what they 'see' and 'hear' instead of dismissing it."

Gill Edwards - from 'Stepping into The Magic'

'SPIRITED'
BY TONY STOCKWELL

This book could easily be dismissed as just another 'celebrity medium's autobiography on the back of some dodgy, hyped-up tv show'. However, I found Tony Stockwell's story to be inspiring. He has both a remarkable gift and a heartfelt desire to help others. He also appears to have remained very focused and down-to-earth despite the bright lights and international travel.

His story is broken up with his own thoughts and observations on certain phenomenon and frequently asked questions. Whilst I do not feel that this is a must-have book, it certainly gives food for thought and an insight into the life of an in-demand medium and 'psychic detective'.

I do feel that this book takes a lot of the hype out of the celebrity status which is given to today's TV mediums. After all, we can only judge them on what makes it to our screens can't we? What really touched me were Tony Stockwell's thoughts in the Epilogue which I feel indicate his true nature and lack of ego; 'My only fear in life - and it is a cross I bear every day - is that I will not accomplish all that I want to accomplish before I come to the end of this particular embodiment"

'Sometimes to get to the fruit of the tree, you have to go out on a limb'

from 'Spirited' by Tony Stockwell

'THE JOURNEY. AN EXTRAORDINARY GUIDE FOR HEALING YOUR LIFE AND SETTING YOURSELF FREE'
BY BRANDON BAYS

"In 1992 Brandon Bays was diagnosed with a football-sized tumour...Only six and a half weeks later she was pronounced textbook perfect - no drugs, no surgery, no tumour. "

A short, easy to read and truly inspiring story. The reader is taken on an emotional journey as Brandon Bays tells her story, not only of her tumour, but other life-challenges that she overcame, and the healing processes that she developed as a result. She tells of many people who have been helped by her meditative processes and the book also includes 'The Journeys' and full instructions so that you too can undergo the transformation.

This book came highly recommended by friends and another friend told me that attending one of 'The Journey' workshops was the most profound experience he had ever undertaken. Well worth a read, whether you are facing a health challenge or not. This book reminds us not only of the amazing healing power of our minds and bodies but who we truly are and the energy, life and positive feelings that we are entitled to enjoy.

"We have always been, and will always be, this pristine flawless diamond"
from 'The Journey' by Brandon Bays

GOAL FREE LIVING
BY STEPHEN SHAPIRO

A fantastic book, not about living completely without goals - they are important to keep us going for our dreams - but about not being so tied up by them that we miss out on living our lives. Find your vision or mission in life and live within that context in everything that you do. Work through the chapters and ask yourself some challenging questions.

"By living for each moment, it's possible to have a successful life and follow your passions at the same time"

Stephen Shapiro

'THE COSMIC ORDERING SERVICE - A GUIDE TO REALIZING YOUR DREAMS'
BY BARBEL MOHR

This book is a simple guide to getting what you want from life. Full of stories and ideas to get you started, even if you're not sure that it will work. Not that well written but easy enough to get through in a short space of time so you can get on and start 'ordering'. After reading this I was re-inspired and placed my order for a particular sum of money and a winning scratch card on return from my holiday. Two days after getting home, I had virtually the exact amount of money in, part of which came from a winning scratch card! (Not that I would recommend gambling, I received the scratch card through a business promotion).

'DON'T KISS THEM GOODBYE'
BY ALLISON DUBOIS

This review was kindly provided by Diane Campkin, co-author of 'Help! I Think I Might Be Psychic'.

This is the intriguing autobiography of Allison Dubois, an American medium who works for her local District Attorney's office.

Allison's amazing gifts were evident from a very young age, although she charts in this book how she was initially frightened and confused by them. There is an interesting section in the book about how to determine whether or not your child has a psychic gift, and how you can encourage and help them to develop it, so that no child has to suffer the fear and confusion that Allison herself did.

Allison also details some of the scientific tests that she has taken part in under the observation of Gary Schwartz, a leading paranormal investigator in the US, and the results leave you in no doubt that she is exceptionally gifted. However the element that I found most interesting was how Allison has used her gift to help solve crimes for the District Attorney's office. From missing persons to murder inquiries, Allison has on many occasions helped justice to prevail. A television series 'Medium' has been created based on her real-life experiences in this field and also makes compelling viewing.

This is an interesting book about a fascinating medium and her remarkable gift. In Allison's own words:-

"Mediums serve people both living and dead.
May this book inspire you as so many have inspired me."

THE LIGHTWORKERS WAY
BY DOREEN VIRTUE

This review was kindly provided by Diane Campkin, co-author of 'Help! I Think I Might Be Psychic'.

Many of us have wondered what our purpose in this lifetime is. Well, this interesting and informative book may have some of the answers. Written by the internationally renowned angel expert, Doreen Virtue, it promises to help you to remember your divine mission and to discover the 'natural spiritual skills that you were born with'.

The book is written in a warm, and at times, searingly honest way, initially charting the author's personal struggles as she seeks her own path to enlightenment. Yet this book is much more than an autobiography. it's also packed with inspirational teachings, practical information, and easy to follow exercises that the reader can try out at home to develop, or hone, their psychic and healing skills. There is also alot of information about discovering your own divine life purpose and how to fulfil it once you have discovered it.

Having read many spiritual books over the years, I found this to be one of the best - it's clear guidance, positive viewpoint, and important messages about manifestation were truly uplifting. It's a must-have for all would be, or practicing, healers and mediums. Put it at the top of your reading wish list today!

'THE SECRET'
BY RHONDA BYRNE

Available as a feature length film on DVD, printed and audio book. (I have this on Audio Book - 4 CD's worth, so that I can listen to it over and over again in the car.)

For many 'the secret' is not new, but for many more, it is. It's simple, joyful and what's more, it works! 'The Secret' centres around the 'law of attraction', that which we send out, we receive. The concept that we can achieve anything in life provided that we think and act in the right way.

The film and book are full of wondrous stories of miraculous healing and people turning their lives around. it's not only a 'how to' for achieving all the things in life that you desire, it's a great vehicle for raising the awareness of spirituality globally and introducing a more spiritual way to many who wouldn't perhaps have considered it before. I would liken it's potential impact to that of 'The Celestine Prophecy' and 'Conversations with God' which both swept the globe with their amazing messages, but possibly even greater.

It transcends cultures and faiths and bridges the gap between spirituality and science by carefully introducing the basics of new discoveries in quantum physics. Leading philosophers, theologians, authors and scientists from around the world give their views and experiences of 'the secret'. Full of great quotes and stories 'The Secret' is extremely thought-provoking, often incredulous, sometimes miraculous but wonderfully inspiring, and it makes me smile too.

'The Secret' needs to be anything but a secret, and in reality it's the essence of what most spiritual teachers are trying to convey to others as we all attempt to 'spread the magic'.

"...begin to understand the hidden untapped power that is within you, and the true magnificence that awaits you in life"

From 'The Secret' by Rhonda Byrne

THE ORACLE OF ILLUMINATION - A MANUAL FOR MANIFESTATION
BY VICKY AND PHILIP ARGYLL

This is possibly one of the most beautiful and inspiring yet simple sets of cards I have seen. Combining powerful colour, symbolism and numerology, these cards seem to connect with your very soul. Even where resistance to the message is felt when reading them, somehow one can still understand their truth, and how it relates to ones journey of life. I found that these cards literally speak on an unheard level. As you work with them you suddenly 'know' or 'feel' the answers, words seem unnecessary. I occasionally found that I had physical reactions to them as my energy body resonated strongly with their powerful messages.

A beautifully written, or should I say 'channelled' book accompanies the cards which gives you ideas and instruction on their use. Use them to help you find insight, resolve conflict, achieve goals, transform your life, manifest your dreams and soul purpose in this incarnation.

I was fortunate enough to meet Vicky Argyll at a local business event and we met up later to find out more about what we are both doing. Vicky gave me a reading with these cards and it was amazing. Vicky and her husband Philip have created, written and published these sets themselves and I think they've done a fantastic job. Vicky speaks from the heart and with the experience of quite literally living the journey of these cards and her passion and purpose come across both in her talk, and in the product itself. For more information, to view other products or to purchase a set of these cards visit Vicky's website: www.wholebeing.org

"The oracle is a gift of love to your soul
and a journey of awakening for your spirit."

Vicky Argyll

PAY IT FORWARD

A great spiritual film with a wonderful message. Starring Haley Joe Osmond, Kevin Spacey and Helen Hunt.

Makes you think, makes you cry, makes you feel that you can make a difference.

ANGEL GUIDANCE BOARD
BY DOREEN VIRTUE

Review kindly provided by Beth Roberts who introduced me to the Angel Board with additional comments from myself and Diane Campkin. Take a look www.local-legend.co.uk for more information on Beth's projects.

This board set is now one of my most prized possessions. It's simple to use, attractively presented and very insightful, as well as great fun (if I dare mention that!) Anyone, from complete novices through to those who are well-practiced at connecting with angels, can get an instant and accurate reading for themselves and others.

The colourful board is set out with twelve clearly defined pathways including Children, Romance, Career and Spiritual Path, as well as one for 'When Will it Happen?' and 'Yes & No' answers. It quickly provides answers and clear guidance to pressing life questions with just a throw of the crystalline dice, whilst focusing on a question in your mind. When you decide which pathway your question relates to, you simply move your marker along the squares on the pathway and the answer is revealed by the one you land on. With practice, of course, you will also gain more expertise at 'reading' your intuitive feelings and impressions for additional information that your own guardian angels provide. The biggest drawback to using the board is that it's completely addictive, so you have to be disciplined with how frequently you put it to use.

I strongly advise keeping a journal of your questions and answers. It's fascinating to review your responses over a few weeks; the important things you need to know are clearly illustrated by the repetition of the same answers.

The board normally retails at £24.99 but do shop around as you can often find it for less.

'Most definitely not a game, but a great tool for use on it's own, or combined with a card reading or even for dowsing over. The uses for this board are multiple and the answers and messages clear, concise and from what we have seen so far, very accurate. I know that I shouldn't be, but I am still amazed when the same answer comes up over and over. I found mine in a bookshop for £15!' - *Helen Leathers*

'Great for beginners and more experienced readers alike.' - *Diane Campkin*

ACKNOWLEDGEMENTS

To my wonderful husband John who puts up with my ramblings on a daily basis, sometimes even more regularly than that, who humours and supports me and allows me to be who I truly am.

To everyone who has helped me in developing my sense of self and of self worth, colleagues, friends, family and very often strangers too.

To Beth and Diane for their belief, love and support and for kindly contributing to the newsletters and allowing me to use their reviews in this book.

To Maxine for helping me out and encouraging me.

To Jane, for inspiring me to write about 'passion' and for helping me to realise my life path. What a relief, I'd been wondering about that for ages!

And with heartfelt thanks to everyone who has subscribed to and given me wonderful feedback on my newsletters.

Bright Blessings to you all.

OTHER PRODUCTS FROM THE AUTHOR

HELP! I THINK I MIGHT BE PSYCHIC –
101 FREQUENTLY ASKED QUESTIONS ABOUT SPIRITUAL, PSYCHIC & SPOOKY STUFF

Answered by Helen Leathers & Diane Campkin

This book is for anyone who has ever asked 'What's it all about?', 'Is there life after death?', 'What's it like to see a ghost?' and other virtually unanswerable questions. Do you have a fascination with or passing interest in the Paranormal?

Do you have a more pressing concern and don't know where to turn for answers?

Do you suspect you have a talent, a path, a dream or desire that you are not fulfilling and you really wish there was more to life?

Whether you have had supernatural experiences or not, this book will give you the basics, and a whole lot more.

This is our take on the often confusing and occasionally, egotistical world of the paranormal. A reference point that's open and honest and that looks to blow away some of the cobwebs surrounding the more esoteric side of life and death, as we see it.

This book is for everyone.

Do you want to know more...?

Order with the form in the back of this book or online at www.helpithinkimightbepsychic.com

RRP £7.95

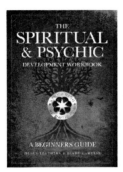

THE SPIRITUAL & PSYCHIC DEVELOPMENT WORKBOOK

A BEGINNERS GUIDE

Helen Leathers & Diane Campkin

An introduction to the theory and practical basics of spiritual and psychic work. This book will facilitate an opening up to and development of your natural spiritual and psychic abilities. This is the book we've been waiting for for years! RRP £9.95

THE SPIRITUAL & PSYCHIC DEVELOPMENT WORKBOOK

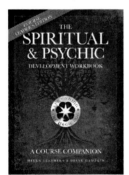

A COURSE COMPANION

Helen Leathers & Diane Campkin

An in-depth course book for workshop leaders, development groups or just a bunch of like-minded friends. A step-by-step guide to running a group, circle or series of workshops on spiritual & psychic development. You don't have to think about it, we've done all the planning for you.

'With these workbooks we will walk and talk you through the process of discovering and developing your own natural abilities.' This workbook is only available direct from Spreadng The Magic. Please take a look at our website for more details.

A4 Spiral Bound for ease of use. £19.95 + P&P

Register for updates and offers on these and find out about future products at:
www.thepsychicworkbook.com
or www.stmpublishing.co.uk

WHAT IS 'SPREADING THE MAGIC'?

Started in 2005 by Helen Leathers, 'Spreading The Magic' began life as an online resource for personal, spiritual and psychic development. Courses and workshops and a small range of products were available. Helen was also writing and had a number of projects on the go at once. But she knew it was extremely difficult to get an agent or publisher in the literary world. So she decided to create what she wanted and pull the two concepts together turning 'Spreading The Magic' into a publisher for her specialist books on the spiritual side of life.

'Spreading The Magic' is a vehicle with which we seek to help others find and develop their own spirituality and integrate it into their daily life.

Our core values are open-mindedness and acceptance.

We want everyone to find their own path and know their own truth. To find the magic in themselves and to see it in others.

The 'magic' is our connection with life, our oneness with the universe and everything within it.

Through our courses, workshops, articles, books, products, websites and events we aim

To encourage, inform and inspire

To simplify and demystify the unknown

To open hearts and minds

To promote non-judgement, acceptance and understanding

To transform and enlighten

To leave a positive impact

To teach others to create their reality

To raise consciousness, personally, socially and globally

To remember

To Be

To spread the magic

Become part of the change at www.spreadingthemagic.com

QUICK ORDER FORM

If you would like any additional copies of this book, or any of our other publications you can:

Buy Online at www.stmpublishing.co.uk

Buy Mail Order – Send this form and appropriate payment to:
Spreading the Magic, Tryfan, Barn Lane, Church Stretton, Shropshire, England SY6 6EB

Please send me .... copies of 'Help! I Think I Might Be Psychic' (£7.95 each)

Please send me .... copies of 'Bright Blessings' (£5.95 each)

Please send me .... copies of 'The Spiritual & Psychic Development Workbook -
A Beginners Guide' (£9.95 each)

P&P (UK)	£2.00 for first book	£1.00 for each subsequent book
P&P (Europe)	£2.50 for first book	£1.50 for each subsequent book
P&P (Rest of World)	£4.00 for first book	£3.00 for each subsequent book

Number of copies: Help! I Think I Might Be Psychic		x £7.95	£
Number of copies: Bright Blessings		x £5.95	£
Number of copies: SPDW A Beginners Guide		x £9.95	£
Postage for your region for first book:	£	x 1	£
Postage for your region for subsequent books:	£	x number of subsequent copies	£
TOTAL:			£

I enclose a cheque for £ .... (sterling only please) made payable to 'SPREADING THE MAGIC'.

YOUR DETAILS:

NAME: ....

ADDRESS: ....

....

....

POSTCODE: .... COUNTRY: ....

TEL NO: .... EMAIL: ....

Please send more FREE information on:

☐ Other Books & Products   ☐ Courses, Workshops, Seminars & Events
☐ By Email   ☐ By Post

We aim to get your books to you within 7 working days of receiving your order, but it may take up to 28 working days, especially if you are ordering from outside of the U.K. Thank you for your patience.

Lightning Source UK Ltd.
Milton Keynes UK

177090UK00003B/76/P